YOU DECIDE

YOU DECIDE

A PRIMER ON DECISION-MAKING

RICK THOMAS

YOU DECIDE:
A Primer on Decision-Making

ISBN 978-1-7323854-2-9

Rick Thomas

© 2025 Life Over Coffee

Unless otherwise noted, all Scripture references herein are from the English Standard Version, copyright © 2001 by Crossway, Inc. Used by permission. All rights reserved.

No part of this publication may be reproduced, stored in a retrieval system, or transmitted in any form or by any means without the express written permission of Life Over Coffee.

Edited by Sarah Hayhurst

Life Over Coffee
8595 Pelham Rd Ste 400 #406,
Greenville, SC 29615
LifeOverCoffee.com

Dedication

To Dave

Dave Forbes was my friend. The Lord called him home in 2024. The Lord used Dave as a primary means for sharing our work with the world.

I miss you, my friend.

For additional resources, visit
lifeovercoffee.com

Table of Contents

Introduction 10
1 How to Make a Bad Decision 16
2 How to Make a Good Decision 26
3 Helpful Decision-Making Tips 38
4 Making Decisions as a Couple 46
5 May I Change My Mind? 56
6 Torment Is Perfection 62

Case Studies 67

7 The Double Minded 68
8 Married the Wrong Person 76
9 Get the Vaccine Already 82
Conclusion 90
About the Author 94

ROMANS 14:23

But whoever has doubts is condemned if he eats, because the eating is not from faith. For whatever does not proceed from faith is sin.

Introduction

God gave everyone an internal moral thermostat, the conscience. Con-science in Latin means co-knowledge, our inner voice. It is one of the means of grace that teaches us how to think and react properly. Along with the Spirit of God, the Word of God, and the people of God, our consciences assist us in the decision-making process that can lead to relational and situational harmony. Of course, a miscalibrated conscience will not do this, choosing instead to be our worst enemy, making it essential to learn how to train our consciences.

Conscience Molding

Biff, a believer, has been living in sin for many years. Though many people have brought his problems to his attention, he has never repented. Typically, Biff reasons along the lines of justifying, rationalizing, or blaming. Sometimes, he alleviates his troubles through alcohol and Internet surfing. The problem for Biff is that his conscience is not neutral but a reactor to his choices. A conscience will react to how we respond to situations in our lives. If we do not respond biblically to sin, our conscience will react by laying down a thin, hard layer over the top of our inner voice, which is what happened to Biff. He is similar to a person who lays in the sun too long. The skin toughens in reaction to the rays. Whether an unrepentant sinner or a sunbather, the result is the same: our sensitivities are altered in unnatural ways.

Depending on how we respond to guilt and conviction, we can soften or harden our inner voice. A tender conscience has a sensitivity to the truth of God's Word. This person wants to walk in line with the gospel, responding promptly and precisely to conviction. The Spirit of God and the inner voice are singing the same tune. Even a temporary transgressor can live in a continual state of love, joy, peace, holiness, and victory if he is a genuine repenter who wants to love God and others more than himself. But if a person chooses to resist repentance, their conscience will take revenge on them. They won't experience the freedom in Christ's work on the cross that removes transgressions. This person will strategize a different way to deal with their sin, which will be a futile attempt, only releasing the conscience to take revenge on the captive soul. Let me explain.

Hard Conscience

When a person is unrepentant, the conscience has no choice but to harden itself. It does this so the transgressor can live with himself. If I repeatedly cut my hand, eventually, it will toughen to the point where I will not be able to feel the pain. A healthy body is supposed to react this way as a form of self-preservation. Our God-given consciences will do a similar thing if the transgressor refuses to repent. The conscience is trying to coexist with a person who refuses to stop harming it. The side-effect is the unrepentant will lose the possibility of having a biblically informed conscience because he desensitized himself to the truth of God's Word (1 Timothy 4:2). One of sin's greatest deceptions is how it blinds the mind from perceiving its dangers. It does this by muting the inner voice, a gift God gave to all people—saved or lost—so they could distinguish truth from error (Romans 2:14–15).

YOU DECIDE

TEN STEP PROCESS TO A HARD HEART
When a desire become a controlling idol

① My desire entices me away from God.

② **IDENTITY**
My desire begins to define me.

③ **UNHAPPY**
My desire overwhelms my joy.

④ **SOUL NOISE**
Discontentment settles in.

⑤ **CYNICISM**
A subtle accusation toward God.

⑥ **CONSCIENCE**
My inner voice starts to dull.

⑦ **GUILT**
I may sense guilt but ignore it.

⑧ **PRIDE**
God is now warring against me.

⑨ **HOPELESS**
My sin is greater than His grace.

⑩ **HARD HEART**
I am blind to my blindness.

But each person is tempted when he is lured and enticed by his own desire. Then desire when it has conceived gives birth to sin, and sin when it is fully grown brings forth death (James 1:14-15).

Tender Conscience

A tender conscience is different from a hard one and not the same as a weak one. A person with a weak conscience, as described in 1 Corinthians 8:1-13, is a person on the opposite end of the spectrum from the hard conscience individual (1 Timothy 4:2). While Biff has rationalized and justified his sin away, the weak conscience person has a longer sin list than God does; many of their perceived sins are not sins at all. For example, in 1 Corinthians 8:1-13, the new converts believed eating meat offered to idols was a sin. Paul said eating meat sacrificed to idols was not wrong. He identified their problem as a weak conscience. They needed conscience retraining to eat meat offered to idols while not experiencing self-imposed self-condemnation for doing something others said was wrong, though God did not. But it was a big deal for these new, weak Christian converts. Sometimes, our families, religious environments, and cultural traditions falsely teach a rigid lifestyle contrary to the Bible. Legalism is rife with a bunch of weak conscience people.

Biblical Conscience

God's Word should inform every conscience how to live well in His world. Our conscience and the Bible should be in the same place when trying to decipher what is actual sin and what is not while responding accordingly. You will never be freer than when your conscience and God's Word sing in tune. Unfortunately, Biff has chosen to ignore the conviction he senses, as informed by the Spirit of God, the Word of God, and his friends. He is using twisted techniques, such as justification, rationalization, blaming, and alleviation to silence his inner voice. Biff thinks that because he can't hear his conscience, he is okay. He is not. Silence is not golden for Biff. God gave him a warning signal, but he has shut it down to the point that he's flying blind, the worst of all human conditions: blind to our blindness.

Call to Action

1. How would you describe your conscience? Is it weak, hard, or biblically informed?
2. Why is understanding your conscience crucial when thinking about decision-making? How can your conscience shape your decision-making ability for good or evil?
3. What have been some of the shaping influences that have trained your conscience for good or evil?
4. If your conscience has adverse shaping influences, what do you need to do now that you know the problem?
5. There are five common ways we alter our consciences. The first is biblical, while the remaining four are damning and distorting: repentance, justification, rationalization, blaming,

and alleviation. Which one of these do you use most often?
6. There are four means of grace to train our conscience correctly
   - Canon: God's Word.
   - Comforter: The Spirit of God
   - Community: Your Friends
   - Conscience: Your Inner Voice
7. How are these four means of grace working for you, and what changes do you need to make so your conscience is more biblically informed, releasing you to have the clarity you need to make decisions?

Most people do not connect their conscience to decision-making, but it is the prerequisite because the clarity or cloudiness of the conscience will establish how we make decisions and set the trajectory and consequences for those decisions. If our conscience is not clear, we cannot be confident that we have made the right decision.

Introduction

1

How to Make a Bad Decision

We will never forget the tragedy of 9/11. Most of us who are old enough remember exactly where we were on that tragic day. I was sitting in my counseling office at our local church, staring blankly at a TV screen as the news unfolded. The best word to describe my mental state was surreal, and it continues to boggle my mind to think how anyone could be so twisted that they would fly a plane into a building and kill 3,000 innocent lives. But then I think of myself in my evil moments of misplaced faith. It's scary. Though none of us will do what those terrorists did, we can go down a regrettable path of hard heartedness and misplaced faith, believing what we're doing is the right thing, begging the question: How can a heart become so hardened that we think what we're doing is okay, even though it's evident to everyone else we're wrong?

Move Forward in Faith

Our entire lives move forward in faith. We do what we do because we believe—a synonym for faith—it is right, whether our motives and methods are right or wrong. Obviously, I'm not talking about biblical faith but a kind of faith that motivates us to move forward because we have a cause, purpose, or agenda that we want to come to fruition. Let me share a few examples of actions we take because we believe—at the moment of insanity—it's the best course of action. I'm not suggesting all these things are the proper moral choices, but all decisions come from a heart that believes it's the right thing to do, even if it's a momentary lapse of judgment or, as James would say, double-mindedness (James 1:5–8).

- It takes faith to choose sinful anger.
- It takes faith to look at porn.
- It takes faith to commit adultery.
- It takes faith to be born again.

> But whoever has doubts is condemned if he eats, because the eating is not from faith. For whatever does not proceed from faith is sin.
> (Romans 14:23)

Paul said it this way, "For whatever does not proceed from faith is sin" (Romans 14:23). Now, before your biblically trained mind blows a head gasket, let me explain. Paul was not thinking about anger, porn, adultery, or flying planes into buildings. He was talking about secondary issues like eating meat, drinking wine, and celebrating certain days. Paul taught his readers that whatever you do, you must do it from a heart of faith: you must believe that your actions are proper. The essence of all decision-making is that all your choices come from a belief system that says it is okay to do what you want to do. Faith to do something—right or wrong—is not Christians' exclusive, hermetically sealed domain. To believe and act on that belief is part of being human. It's how our minds operate: we think and act on what we believe to be the best path forward.

YOU DECIDE

Our Moral Thermostat

We move forward in faith because we have removed doubt, which releases us to do what we do with the confidence that it's right. The problem is that we will make the wrong decision if we base the doubt-removing process on skewed presuppositions and erroneous data; we believe it's right, though the Bible forbids such things. Mercifully, God gave us an internal moral thermostat that helps us guard against acting with wrong presuppositions and insufficient data. We can discern between right and wrong, even if we're not Christians. Our conscience is our inner voice that monitors and directs all of our actions.

> For when Gentiles, who do not have the law, by nature do what the law requires, they are a law to themselves, even though they do not have the law. They show that the work of the law is written on their hearts, while their conscience also bears witness, and their conflicting thoughts accuse or even excuse them.
> (Romans 2:14–15)

The conscience is one of the soul's most essential components because it governs how we think about and respond to good and evil. Our conscience can accuse us, or it can excuse us. What Paul had in view in Romans is a people group who did not know about the Old Testament. They did not have a Bible. They did not know God through special revelation (Romans 10:17). Though they did not accept the Bible's truth claims, they did possess a moral thermostat that convinced them of right and wrong actions. This means of common grace to all of humanity is one of the most compelling reasons why none of us will have an excuse if we choose to reject Christ (Romans 1:20–21). Regardless of a person's relationship with Christianity, everyone is born with an internal wiring system that enables them to discern right from wrong. Even a child knows the difference between right and wrong.

A Bendable Conscience

Paul elevated the importance of the conscience, a warning that should motivate us not to tinker with another person's thermostat unwisely. The implication is clear: the conscience is malleable. A person will be in moral trouble if he bends his thermostat outside biblical parameters. We see this moldable possibility in Paul's letter to Timothy. He called it the seared or hardened conscience. Do you see what happened to those people who had hard consciences? Once their consciences became calloused, they could do all sorts of evil practices because a hardened conscience ceases to condemn of wrongdoing. A hardened conscience is like a callused hand—it feels no pain.

> Now the Spirit expressly says that in later times, some will depart from the faith by devoting themselves to deceitful spirits and teachings of demons, through the insincerity of liars whose consciences are seared, who forbid marriage and require abstinence from foods that God created to be received with thanksgiving by those who believe and know the truth.
> (1 Timothy 4:1-3)

If the conscience is not brought under the clarity and scrutiny of God's Word (Hebrews 4:12-13; 1 Timothy 3:16-17), in the context of a biblical community (Hebrews 10:24-25), as illuminated by the Spirit of God (John 16:13), it will harden. Paul knew we had to handle our consciences with the utmost care, which is why he talked about never eating meat in front of a person whose conscience accused them of wrongdoing; they believed it was wrong to eat what was offered to idols (1 Corinthians 8:13). Paul aimed to use wise and practical love (1 Corinthians 8:1-2) when engaging those with a miscalibrated conscience.

Life Flows from Faith

Paul taught how old Jewish traditions trained newly-minted Christian believers. He also appealed to Christians in Ephesus to change some of their ways—practices born out of old belief systems—that kept them entangled in a former manner of living (Ephesians 4:22). These young converts in Corinth and Ephesus still had faith in ideas that were not biblically sound (1 Corinthians 8:1-13). They had misplaced faith, but it was faith nonetheless. Faith is about what you believe is right, regardless of how that belief lines up with God's Word. The man will only fly an airplane into a building because he believes his action is correct. He has misinformed faith to do an ungodly atrocity. He is acting out of and proceeding from a twisted belief system.

We understand how a terrorist will commit terror, but what if we make it more practical since none of us will fly a plane into a building? Did you know we act according to our faith when choosing sinful anger toward someone? We believe it is right to do in that moment of heretical madness (James 1:5-8). When we're in our sin-filled anger episode, we have convinced—another word for faith—ourselves that we are right, and based on that false belief, we respond accordingly. What we believe—as shown by our anger—and what the Bible teaches are at odds. After choosing sinful anger, the most important thing we can do is recalibrate our beliefs to biblical faith. The worst thing we could do is to validate our conscience through blame-shifting, justifications, or rationalizations.

A New Moral Standard

If we do not recalibrate our conscience to the teaching of God's Word, we will alter our moral thermostat to a new ethical standard that will begin to condone sinful anger. The man who flew the plane into a building needed to adjust his deceitful belief system to God's Word rather than a belief system that condoned such brutality. Regrettably, he calibrated his conscience to a pagan belief system, ignoring a God-given conscience and His inspired Word. It did not seem odd to him to kill 3,000 innocent people or to take his own life. This tragedy begs a few questions for us to ponder and apply.

- How are we similar to him?
- How have we convinced (faith) ourselves that our actions are correct?
- How many times have we justified what we did?

On a few occasions, when I have vented anger toward my wife, I immediately started recalibrating my conscience to an alternate belief system—my way versus the Bible's way—by justifying my actions. This recalibration process permits me to blame my actions on her or something else. Initially, my conscience would blare at me, telling me to stop being angry at my wife. A biblically informed conscience should do this, which is the beauty of God's Word when the Spirit illuminates the mind. The perfect sweet spot is when our conscience—an internal, moral belief system—and God's Word are aligned.

Because I chose to make my conscience incongruent with God's Word in the moment of sinful anger, my conscience flexed and adapted to my new morality. This new morality permits me to be angry, believing it is okay to be mad without remorse or repentance. If we do not bring our conscience under the Word's surveillance and sovereign management, it will drift from the truth while adapting to a rogue reality and seal itself—harden—into that new belief system. At that point, we will act according to our newly minted, albeit evil, belief system.

The Hardening Process

> *Therefore, as the Holy Spirit says, "Today, if you hear his voice, do not harden your hearts as in the rebellion, on the day of testing in the wilderness."*
> *(Hebrews 3:7-8)*

The misguided Muslim, who wants to kill people, has a different faith. It is a faith steeped in hatred for anyone unlike him. His conscience does not condemn him because he has saturated his conscience in an evil belief system. We see this idea in our country every day.

- Those who hate blacks are like this Muslim.
- Those who hate whites are like this Muslim.
- Those who hate gays are like this Muslim.
- Those who hate Christians are like this Muslim.
- Those who hate the other political party are like this Muslim.
- Those who hate their spouses are like this Muslim.

This kind of faith is born from sinful heart cravings (James 4:1-3). People like this blind themselves to the truth of God's Word by embracing another truth while affirming their actions as right. Their rightness and the Bible's rightness live incongruently, but they are free to do as they please because their consciences do not condemn them. It's sobering to think how we can desensitize our consciences to such a degree that we can't sense the immorality we perpetrate on others.

Silencing the Conscience

This hardening concept is what happens to the porn addict. Perhaps the first time he did porn, he felt a twinge of guilt. Maybe he repented or tried to repent, but he was unwilling to go all the way by letting others know about his sin. Rather than exposing his sin's complexity to God's sanitizing light (1 John 1:7–10), he went through a private repentance process that did not altogether pull his conscience in line with God's Word. This half-hearted process of worldly sorrow put down a thin layer of hardness over his inner voice. After looking at porn and masturbating a few more times, the condemnation began to subside. Perhaps he convinced himself by the intellectually dishonest argument that it was okay to masturbate. Or, maybe he blamed his wife because she was unwilling to have sex with him.

Whatever his reasons were, they all served the same purpose: to harden his conscience to the point where he could look at porn, masturbate, and not feel bad about what he was doing. He created a new belief system in his psyche (soul), an aberrant faith. His unique-to-him and adjusted faith made him free and clear to do porn. His moral thermostat went utterly off the biblical grid, and he could not or would not (probably a combination of both) see the truth. An addict is a man who is in full-tilt self-deception. If we do not feel deep conviction and personal brokenness over our sin (see Psalms 32 and 51), one of the most productive things we could do is let others know about our sin. Our conscience is too distorted to see what is happening, and our will is too weak to do anything about it. We need a competent, compassionate, and courageous friend.

Sin will capture us (Galatians 6:1). In such cases, our problem is more than behavioral sinning. The deeper sin I'm talking about is the deception that is going on inside us. Our deceit is more complicated than the behavioral sin committed. There is probably nothing more frightening than living life while blind to the deceptiveness of the heart. My appeal to anyone is not to play around with this. Paul had a high view of conscience. There is a reason his language sounded hyperbolic in 1 Corinthians 8:13. To fool around with the conscience is a matter of life and death. Our conscience is our highest level of morality, and if it is not in line with the Word of God, we may be able to live with ourselves because we have readjusted it, but others will have a hard time living with us.

> Therefore, if food makes my brother stumble, I will never eat meat, lest I make my brother stumble.
> (1 Corinthians 8:13)

Call to Action

If there is any sense that you may be hardening your conscience, will you share the truth about yourself with others? Will you let others speak into your life? Let others help you readjust your conscience to biblical clarity and norms. One of our *Mastermind Students* was thinking about these things and responded by giving me an instructive step-by-step analysis of how we can warp our consciences and put things back on track. Will you spend time reflecting on this progression?

1. I have a good desire for intimacy with my spouse.
2. If I respond to my craving on my terms, it becomes an evil desire.
3. I see a shapely figure that looks appealing.
4. I choose to gaze and lust after her.
5. My conscience tells me that I am morally wrong.
6. I justify actions.
7. In time, a hardening process of my conscience begins.

8. By justifying my actions, I become convinced I am doing nothing wrong and continue my sin.
9. If I do not recalibrate my conscience, I will continue my sin.
10. I am now operating out of a new, though false, belief system.
11. I read my Bible and feel conviction.
12. My conscience begins to recalibrate by responding correctly to God.
13. I confess my sins and begin the repentance process.
14. I'm now turning from my sin.
15. I continue putting off old habits while hoping to put on new ones (Ephesians 4:22–24).
16. I must continually be in the Word of God to have a biblically informed conscience.
17. I must have ongoing care and accountability to avoid being deceived like this again.

2

How to Make a Good Decision

When deciding anything, you must be in faith regarding that decision, which is why the most important question you will ever ask yourself when making a decision is, "Am I in faith to (insert the thing you're thinking about) to do this?" Thus, having a biblically informed conscience that does not obscure your presuppositional lens will help you to see the facts clearly, and it will give you the best shot at making the most God-honoring decision.

When in Doubt

> But whoever has doubts is condemned if he eats, because the eating is not from faith. For whatever does not proceed from faith is sin.
> (Romans 14:23)

I told my friend that when deciding anything, you must be in faith regarding that decision. My friend responded by asking what I meant when I said that you must be in faith before you can move forward with a decision. The term in faith comes from Paul's language in Romans 14:23. He was saying that all of our decisions must go forth from a heart of faith. Maybe a few synonyms will help you to bring more color to the word faith: trust, belief, hope, or confidence. Here are a few sample questions to ask yourself when working through the process of biblical decision-making. You'll notice that these are five ways of asking the same thing.

- Are you in faith to proceed with marriage to your girlfriend?
- Are you trusting the Lord to proceed with marriage?
- Do you believe marrying this person is the right thing for you?
- Is your hope in the Lord as you move forward with marriage?
- Is your confidence resting in the Lord, releasing you to proceed in marrying this person?

All of these questions ask one thing: Are you in faith to get married? I chose to use the term in faith because it is how Paul appealed to the Romans to think about their decision-making. My friend was in the process of deciding to marry someone, which is why I asked him if he was in faith to move forward—to proceed with marrying his girlfriend. I wanted to know if he was confident that God wanted him to do that. We spent the next hour or so unpacking how to grow in faith while addressing some of the ancillary pitfalls of biblical decision-making. While I cannot recreate that discussion in its totality here, I do want to present some of the most critical points that we discussed, which are essential for any couple thinking about marriage.

YOU DECIDE

Making a Decision

Biff and Mable are thinking about marriage. I asked Biff if he was in faith for this new adventure with his soon-to-be new bride. A Christian's life is born out of and proceeds from a life of faith (Romans 1:17; Hebrews 11:6). Our decision to trust God is by faith. Our decision to marry is by faith. Our decision to eat at that (restaurant) is by faith. Our decision not to sin is based on faith: You believe it is wrong to (insert the sin here). In the context of this discussion on decision-making, being in faith means that what you are doing is the right thing for you to do. It implies that you are confident the Lord wants you to do what you are about to do.

This kind of decision-making applies to the simplest things in life as well as to the more complex decisions you must make to live well in God's world. Biff and Mable's decision is one of those more complex life choices. Participating in the interactive adventure of marriage is one of the top three spheres in which we operate. Family, work, and church is where most Christians spend the bulk of their lives. You will not wrestle as much about whether you should eat at McDonald's or Burger King or have a meal at home, but you will spend considerably more time growing in faith for a future spouse, the one you believe God wants you to marry.

Four-Legged Decision

Faith is like a stool upon which we sit. That stool has four legs: Canon, community, conscience, and Comforter. If you place yourself in a context where these four means of grace give you sound advice, you will probably be safe to move forward in faith with what you want to do. The beauty of this fourfold aspect of decision-making is how they balance each other. It helps us not to misuse or misapply one aspect over the other.

- **CANON:** What does the Bible say about getting married? (2 Timothy 3:16–17)
- **COMMUNITY:** What do a few trusted, courageous, and wise friends say about you marrying this person? (Proverbs 11:14)
- **CONSCIENCE:** What do you think about getting married to this person? (Romans 2:14–15)
- **COMFORTER:** What does the Spirit of God say about you marrying? (John 16:13)

Most poor decisions happen because the person who made the decision was not benefiting from these four powerful means of grace the Lord provides for us. They either did not know about this process or, even more sinister, they did not want to hear what God and others had to say to them. One of the marks of humility is holding one's ideas loosely while submitting them to God's Word and His community for more careful analysis. This worldview reminds me of a time when I became angry at our daughter.

After I lashed out at her and after she had slithered back to her room, I asked Lucia if she felt that I was too harsh with her. I was not asking because I was humble. I was asking, hoping that Lucia would side with my evil motives by saying that I was not unkind to our daughter. The truth was that I did not want to know the truth. I was hoping to be justified in my sin, altering my conscience by exchanging the truth for a lie. Mercifully, Lucia did not side with my sinister motives, but admonished me in a loving but firm way by saying I was wrong in the way I treated our child.

There are times when we know what we should do, but we don't want to do it (James 4:17). We can be so deceptive that we do not want to submit our ideas to others because they may not side with us. We can be even more deceptive when we present our thoughts to individuals whom we know will not have the courage or the wisdom to counter what we want. We pick certain people who have no potential or courage to offer an alternate opinion. Such a person is not looking for God's thoughts on the matter. They are seeking a way to justify what they have already determined to do, and they go the extra mile by finding people who agree with them.

Distancing from the Truth

This deception has immediate and long-term results. The direct result is that you can get what you want. The long-term effects are twofold:

- The outcome will not be as you hoped.
- Your unwillingness to cooperate with God will complicate your life when inevitable disappointment comes. (James 4:6 – God resists the proud.)

Additionally, suppose you continue to deceive people to

accomplish selfish goals. In that case, you will eventually harden your conscience, which will make it more difficult in the future for you to perceive God's truth and direction for your life (Hebrews 3:7-8). Individuals who want to manipulate people and situations rarely consider this second point because they want to fulfill their desires. They do not understand that when you alter God's truth, there is a proportional adverse effect on the conscience (Romans 1:18). The conscience is our moral thermostat that God gave to us to alert us of right and wrong. Even the non-Christian has this gift from the Lord (Romans 2:14-15). Problems happen when we tweak our moral thermostats through justifications, rationalizations, blame-shifting, or alleviation—the four main ways we alter God's truth. As we do this, it creates a hardening effect on the conscience (1 Timothy 4:2).

- **JUSTIFICATION:** Pronouncing my actions as not guilty, regardless of what the Bible says about them.
- **RATIONALIZATION:** Comparing what I did with others by minimizing the wrongness while creating tolerance for doing what I want to do.
- **BLAMING:** Rather than perceiving and acknowledging my wrongness, I blame others for what went wrong. I refuse to own my sin.
- **ALLEVIATION:** Seeking escape mechanisms to numb my mental state, helping me not to think about what the Bible says I should do.

If your conscience, like a thermostat, is altered, it will not give you an accurate reading. It may be 100 degrees in your home, but the thermostat says everything is fine. A conscience manipulated is worse than useless. It's dangerous. The more you mute your conscience, the more distance you will put between yourself, God's Word, His community, and the Spirit's illuminating power. You will become more and more isolated from the truth with no inner voice to persuade you otherwise.

- **Canon:** Will you humbly seek God's Word to find the answers to your questions about marriage?
- **Community:** Will you humbly place your marriage desires in the hands of trusted, wise, and courageous friends who will not automatically tell you what you want to hear?
- **Conscience:** Will you not only listen to what your inner voice is telling you, but will you respond to it—assuming your conscience is in line with God's Word?
- **Comforter:** Will you honestly say you have not exchanged the truth of God for a lie because you have submitted your desires for marriage to scrutiny through the means of the Canon of God's Word, the community of God's children, your conscience, and the Holy Spirit?

Therefore God gave them up in the lusts of their hearts to impurity, to the dishonoring of their bodies among themselves, because they exchanged the truth about God for a lie and worshiped and served the creature rather than the Creator, who is blessed forever! Amen.

(Romans 1:24)

Expect Disappointment

One of the more instructive things I have seen about decision-making is that after we make a decision and proceed in faith, we forget to factor in future disappointment. It is like we don't remember how our lives are called to suffer (1 Peter 2:21). You may recall that on a dark and stormy night, the Lord asked Peter to step off a boat and walk on water. Peter did as he was asked to do (Matthew 14:28–36).

He stepped off the vessel and proceeded in faith, probably believing it was going to turn out well for him. After Peter had walked a few steps on the water, he began to notice the waves and the wind. He quickly forgot who called him as his faith shifted from the Lord to the waves. What he could see and experience was more influential to him than the Lord (2 Corinthians 5:7). Aren't we like this? We pray. We seek counsel. We move forward in faith. Then all hell breaks loose, and we lose faith in the process.

A lack of biblical faith is what the Lord rebuked Peter for after they returned to the safety of the boat: "O you of little faith, why did you doubt?" (Matthew 14:31). Let me go ahead and state the obvious: no matter what your decision is, after you move forward with your plans, you will be disappointed in some way, whether small or large. One of the more recurring applications of the gospel is how the Lord uses the process of dying to ourselves to accomplish His purposes in our lives and relationships (Matthew 16:24–26; 2 Corinthians 1:8–9). At times, we can think more like spoiled, first-world people than like Christians. We embrace the happily-ever-after worldview, which is biblical in a sense: we will be happy forever in eternity (Revelation 21:4), but that is not our reality for the here and now.

If you smuggle in the notion that your decision to marry someone is more about your happiness than God's glory, you will surely be set up for disappointment. Plus, you will live in doubt, regret, bitterness, and anger as you think about your past decisions. Self-preservation must not be the driving theme of your decision-making. While you should not be foolish by blindly jumping off a cliff, you must not err the other way by trying to insulate all your decisions from potential suffering.

Purposeful Freedom

Sometimes, God gives us multiple options to choose from, none of which are necessarily wrong. For example, it might not be wrong to eat at McDonald's or Burger King or home. Decision-making does not have to be like an archer standing 100 yards from a target with one arrow trying to hit the bull's eye. If you follow the steps outlined in this chapter, you may come to the end of the process with multiple choices from which to choose your future mate. Maybe you want to go on a vacation, and you land on two options: the mountains or the beach. Perhaps there are two potential marriage partner options. They both fit within the four-legged stool metaphor.

- **Canon:** The Bible does not prohibit either one.
- **Community:** Your close friends weigh in, and they see no problem with either one.
- **Conscience:** Your conscience is free on the matter.
- **Comforter:** It appears there is no quenching or grieving of the Spirit with either choice (Ephesians 4:10; 1 Thessalonians 5:19).

If you are free and clear, then you may choose one or the other. In the case of a vacation, you may want to do both—an option that is not available when selecting a mate. You should not sweat your decision. Be free. Where sin is not involved because your conscience is clear, choose while rejoicing in God's kindness to give you more than one option. Just before I met Lucia, I had gone out with another girl. Suddenly, I had two girls in my life. After going through this process, it proved that it was not wrong to continue seeing either one of them. Then, I made a fabulous choice.

Call to Action

1. Are you sure the Lord wants you to marry that person?
2. Are you holding your desires for marriage loosely while submitting them to others?
3. Do you want to know the truth, and are you humbly seeking answers—specifically from competent people who do not always agree with you?
4. Is your motive for marriage more about God's glory than selfish desires? How do you know?
5. How much does self-protection or self-preservation influence your decision-making? How much does foolish thinking impact your decision to marry?

YOU DECIDE

To the Premarital Counselor

There is one question that transcends all other matters in premarital counseling. It is this: "Are you sure, confident, or in faith that you are to marry this person?" The reason that question is the most important one is that there will come a time in this couple's future marriage when bad things will happen to them. They may lose their home or a job, become bankrupt, develop a lifetime disability, discover a life-dominating sin, have a miscarriage, or learn hurtful things about their spouse that were not evident while dating. They will become older and change in many ways. They will not be the same people that they were while dating.

There may be a time when most of the reasons they had for their marriage and the things they liked about being married go away. If that is the case, there must be one thing left: they believed God wanted them to marry each other. It is essential that all premarital counseling walks through this concept of biblical decision-making while exploring the couple's reasons, motives, and agendas for marriage. They will more than likely tell you that they are in faith to move forward to matrimony. Do not be deterred: you must explore their motives, reasons, desires, and dreams. The couple must know that being married to each other is the right thing to do, or as Paul said, they must move forward in faith.

How to Make a Good Decision

3

Helpful Decision-Making Tips

Every day, you have to make many decisions, big and small. Some of them are life-changing events, while others aren't as consequential. It would shock many of us to realize how often we're deciding things. From micro-decisions, those subtle, silent decisions, to life and family-altering decisions, having a good grasp of biblical decision-making is vital. I have a decision-making case study and a few practical guidelines that will serve you in all of the decisions that you have to make.

Case Study

Biff and Mable are in love. They have been talking about getting married for a while. They love God, have been pure in their relationship, and want to honor their parents. They met in college but have waited until both have secured good jobs and paid off most of their college debt. They have known each other for five years and have dated for the past 18 months. They come to you for counsel. While they are confident that they will marry, and both sets of parents are okay with the idea, they want your thoughts about a potential engagement and future union.

You have a list of questions you want to ask them, but

there is one that is more critical than the rest. And it is the first one that you ask Biff and Mable. What is the question you want to ask them, and why is it more important than the others? Based on the previous chapter, I'm sure you have the answer, but for this chapter, I want you to add another dimension: How do you make it practical? This case study will explore your understanding of decision-making while giving you a few practical guidelines for making decisions.

You Must Be "In Faith"

The most critical question you want to ask Biff and Mable is, "Are you in faith to get married?" Or, stated another way, "Do you have a 'word from the Lord' that you are supposed to marry this person?" You could also query them by asking, "Do you believe this is God's will for your life?" All three of my questions are the same, and they cause you to explore whether or not you're walking in faith as you embark on whatever it is that you hope to do. It does not matter exactly how you ask the in faith question, as long as you do and explain why you're asking the question. When it comes to biblical decision-making, there is no more important question that you can ask.

Granted, in this case study, it will hardly matter to Biff and Mable. In nearly all cases where folks are in love, it does not matter what you say to them because they already know it's God's will, and they are on the right path. They will answer your questions in the affirmative. Most young couples are so enamored with one another that all objectivity is out the window. Nevertheless, it would be best if you had a conversation with them about the faith factor because what you know is that there will come a day when they will wonder why they married each other.

Whatever Is Not of Faith

But whoever has doubts is condemned if he eats, because the eating is not from faith. For whatever does not proceed from faith is sin.

(Romans 14:23)

When Paul talked about making decisions, he connected whatever we decide to our being in faith. His language was strong and clear. He said that if we did not make our decisions from faith, we would be sinning. A modern paraphrase of Paul's verse is "When in doubt, don't." Paul says that it is a sin to proceed into any situation if we cannot move forward, knowing we are doing the right thing. Biff and Mable must trust God as it pertains to their future and potential marriage. They must believe that marriage is God's will for them. They must be in faith.

Common Decision-Making Questions

Here are four typical questions about biblical decision-making.

- Why do you say this is the most critical question? This entire chapter, plus the prior chapter, answers that question.
- Does this mean I can't doubt at all? Are you talking about perfect faith before I can make a decision?
- What if I married a person, but now I realize I was not in faith when we were married, and now our marriage stinks? What am I to do now?
- How can I know God's will? Can you give me details on how to make decisions in faith?

A Few Practical Guidelines

- **No Perfect Decisions:** Some people can be so measured, calculating, and fearful that they cannot decide until all fear, doubt, and worry are gone. Sometimes, these people are self-righteous; they want to look good in front of others. Failure is not an option, so rather than pushing forward, they make excuses and wait. Caution is wise, but paralysis is not. There aren't any perfect decisions where you will be 100% sure without any reservations that you've done the right thing. Faith does not work that way. If you had all the answers before you moved forward, you would not be operating in faith but moving forward because of the known outcome.
- **Impulsiveness:** The other side of paralysis is the self-sufficient person who devalues the community and the other means of grace that God has given to help guide him. Close friends or wise counselors should influence the decisions that matter. A humble person always carries a sense of self-suspicion. However, rather than that awareness leading to paralysis, it motivates them to borrow brains. They want to gain the perspective of others so they can do proper due diligence. The gospel-centered person has nothing to fear, hide, or protect. He is humble, open to correction, and willing to seek the wisdom of other like-minded individuals.
- **Asking True Friends:** There may be a temptation to ask only those who agree with you or those who do not have the grace to disagree with you. A true friend will tell you what you might not want to hear. "Faithful are the wounds of a friend; profuse are the kisses of an enemy" (Proverbs 27:6) is an excellent

verse to practicalize. Don't surround yourself with yes people. What good is that? Living in an echo chamber with folks who are not willing to disagree with you is not how you sharpen your iron (Proverbs 27:17).

- **Guard Against Being Offended:** It is a definite sign of Christian maturity to receive correction with grace. Too often, the focus is on how the correction came rather than the truth that the person shared. Perhaps they were 90% wrong in delivery and 10% correct with the truth. For the need to make the right decision, the most vital thing is to hear the truth proclaimed. Perhaps you can talk about the delivery later. It's easy to focus so much on the desire to be right that we miss God's corrective care through the imperfect people who bring their perspectives. Thus, guard against being offended while opening yourself up to another view.
- **Telling But Not Asking for Help:** There have been a few times in my life when someone has come to me and told me what he had planned to do. Then they asked me what I thought about what they had already decided. Here are a few of those scenarios.

- Hey Rick, we just put our house on the market, and we're moving to Vermont. What do you think?
- I just gave my boss a two-week notice. Is that a good idea?
- Yesterday, I borrowed a thousand bucks for our family vacation. Do you think that was wise?

Don't do this to your friends because you will put them in an awkward position. Most of the time, particularly if I don't know them well, I won't tell them what I think. They have already decided, and my perspective won't make any difference. They are telling me what they have done rather than asking me what I think about what they would like to do.

Remember the Letter "V"

I use the illustration of a "V" when making this point. The letter "V" is narrow at the bottom and broad at the top. The illustration means you have a defined starting point, but there are many possible ending points. But if you flip the "V" upside down, there is a predetermined point at the top with no other options. I have seen many people flip the "V" upside down, and through hell or high water, they were going to get to their predetermined destination. For example, a young man wants to go into the ministry, but he's not qualified to do so. After careful evaluation, several individuals concur that he does not have the gift mix for what he wants to do, but the preacher wannabe has already determined the outcome; he is going to be a preacher.

Wannabe biblical counselors will make this mistake, too. They have a desire to be a counselor and conjure up a false continuum formula in their minds: a burden equals a calling, which is not always true. Many times, these people are driven more by selfish ambition rather than by an actual call from God. The big idea here is to hold your narrative loosely. There could be broader possibilities for God's plans for your life. You should say, "If the Lord wills, I can do this or that" (James 4:13-17). If you predetermine how your decision should turn out, you may live in perpetual disappointment. There are many instances in Scripture where someone made a decision, and the outcome was dismal, despairing, and deathly. Read Hebrews 11. Sometimes, the choice you make in faith leads to hard times, and that is God's will for your life. Read 2 Corinthians 1:8-9.

You Can Change Your Mind

Decision-making is an imperfect science because we're fallen individuals. There are times when you make a decision and then realize it was not the best idea, so you change your mind and the direction of your life. It is best to make these decisions in the context of the Canon, Comforter, community, and your conscience—the Bible, Spirit, friends, and what you believe in your heart of hearts. Perhaps your decision led you into hardship, and that is supposed to be your lot in life. Alternatively, it led to difficulty, and you should change your plans. Each situation is unique and requires the utmost patience, wisdom, humility, and careful assessment before you change your mind and life trajectory. It's not wrong to change your plans, but you want to make sure that you have weighed what you're thinking carefully, using the means of grace provided by God: Canon, Comforter, community, and conscience.

You Must Be In Faith

Ultimately, we must be in faith to make or change a decision. The biggest pitfall of all is not having faith in what we are about to do. Usually, it's other things that are at the top of the list for why we do what we do. For example, some of the wrong reasons for married couples are that they are in love, meant for each other, or it feels right. While all those things are great, they cannot be at the top of their decision-making process list. When all the secondary and tertiary reasons fade, they want one thing to stand tall, and that is their belief that God was leading them. They were in faith to proceed.

Call to Action

1. How do you describe your decision-making? Impulsive, paralysis, anxious, confident, etc.? What does your answer reveal about your relationship with God?
2. When did you make a wrongheaded decision? What was wrong about it, and how did it play out? How did God use a bad decision to bring about good?
3. Have you ever made a decision only to realize later that you needed to make a change? How did that go?
4. Do you live in regret for some of your past decisions? If so, why do you? What does ongoing regret reveal about your relationship with God and His sovereignty?

4

Making Decisions as a Couple

Biblical decision-making is not that difficult if you are the only one making the decision. There are challenges, of course, but it's much easier if you're the only one affected by the decision you make. Once the number of contributors to the decision-making process increases and the consequences are broader, it will be more challenging to navigate with humility, clarity, and mutually agreed-upon cooperation regarding the path forward. Having guidelines for couples and friends is crucial.

Welcome to Marriage

When two singles become one flesh, decision-making changes dramatically. Because the married couple is one person in covenant, seeking to put Christ on display in every way, they must work through the process with God-glorifying goals in mind. They are partners, equally responsible to each other and to God for what they decide and for how they make decisions. In this chapter, I will provide a few general and biblical guidelines that can serve any couple when they are making a decision. If you are not married, you can use these concepts by adapting my application questions with anyone who is collaborating with you on a decision. I recommend you take the time to answer all of the questions after each section. If you are married, it will be an excellent opportunity for you to work together, perhaps something for a great date night.

You Cannot Sin

Regardless of the issues discussed or the particulars involved in the decision, there is no situation where it would be appropriate for either partner to sin during or after the process. This mandate is not only common sense, but it's biblical. Once sin infringes on what you're trying to do, you will have a hard time coming to the right decision until the blurring effect of the sin is removed. Sin clutters the mind and clouds judgment. It cannot be part of the process. If a spouse chooses to sin, the most immediate item on the agenda is to work toward a process of repentance.

Removing the sin is more critical than the decision you're attempting to make. You should not move forward until you take care of the division that is in your one-flesh union. Two people cannot work together on anything while divided. You must fully restore the one-flesh division so you can get back to the business of decision-making. If someone chooses not to repent, it will be even more difficult to make progress. This outcome of one-flesh disunity creates three problems where only one previously existed:

- **PROBLEM ONE:** The decision you were trying to make.
- **PROBLEM TWO:** The introduction of sin into the conversation, which divided you.
- **PROBLEM THREE:** The lack of full repentance keeps you divided.

Refusing to discuss what has divided the couple is called a complicating matter—it piles on or complicates the decision-making process. If it is not removed, it could be analogous to trying to swim with leg weights around the ankles.

- Are you working through a decision in your marriage?
- Are there any tensions or unresolved issues between you and your spouse? What about unforgiveness?
- Can you bring up your tension and get things out in the open?
- Are you generally characterized as a quick and willing repenter? If not, why not?

Decisions Should Not Take Long

Why do you see the speck that is in your brother's eye, but do not notice the log that is in your own eye? Or how can you say to your brother, "Let me take the speck out of your eye," when there is the log in your own eye? You hypocrite, first take the log out of your own eye, and then you will see clearly to take the speck out of your brother's eye.

(Matthew 7:3–5)

There could be something wrong with a relationship if it takes a long time to come to a decision. Perhaps you're not going to act on what you decided for a few months or even years, but the actual decision-making process should not take that long after you have all the data. Furthermore, if someone is holding out by refusing to agree, it does not necessarily mean the hesitant spouse is wrong. Maybe the one who wants to move forward is wrong, and the one holding out is in the right. Holding out and not moving forward sometimes can be God's kindness to the one who wants to get on with it. Perhaps God is keeping the couple from making a dumb decision that they would regret for many years to come. Jesus's sober warning in Matthew 7:3–

5 about self-awareness is critical.
- How difficult is it for you to acknowledge that you were wrong?
- Are you willing to entertain the thought that your spouse could be right?
- Can you clearly articulate your spouse's position? Do you understand what they are thinking or saying?
- What are a few of the positive points about the other person's position?

Borrow Brains

Where there is no guidance, a people falls, but in an abundance of counselors there is safety.
(Proverbs 11:14)

While there can be confusion in a multitude of counselors, there most certainly can be safety if you choose to talk to someone outside of your marriage. Every person (or couple) should have at least one other person that they can bounce things off of for clarity's sake. Helping people with problems is what God has called all Christians to do for each other. Though you would not necessarily ask for advice on everything you do, it is definitely a humble thing to reach out to someone who has the wisdom and breadth of knowledge to speak into your life.

- Do you have a trusted friend who can advise you on your decision?
- What are the advantages of talking to someone else about your decision?
- What would hinder you from talking to someone else?
- If you don't have a trusted friend, why not?

The Husband Is Not a Dictator

The husband and wife are a team that balances each other out for God's glory and their mutual benefit. There have been many times when my wife has appealed to me because her conscience was not coming to terms with some of the decisions that I was thinking about making. In those situations, I listened to her appeals for many reasons.

- She is a Christian.
- She loves God.
- She has the Spirit of God inside her.
- She reads her Bible.
- She has a vibrant relationship with Jesus Christ.
- She knows Him; He knows her, and they relate well to each other.
- She possesses gifts of the Spirit that I do not have.

The things the Spirit has given to me are not identical to what He has given to her, which is why I do not see her as an irritating appendage to our marriage. Lucia is an instrumental asset to the Lord's work in our lives. She is my most valuable ally, and I trust her walk with God and the wisdom He gives her. I want to know what she is hearing from the Lord.

- Does your spouse have a relationship with God?
- Are you willing to tap into that relationship and learn what God is revealing to your partner?
- Are you willing to accept the possibility that God may be leading your spouse in the right decision?
- Are you more concerned with being right, or are you more concerned about discerning God's perspective regardless of who came up with the idea?

The Wife Is Not a Doormat

The wife can and should make a humble appeal to her husband when she believes—at a conscience level—that her husband may be making a poor decision. There is no such teaching in Scripture that a wife is to submit to her husband in everything, though some misinterpret the word everything in Ephesians 5:24. For example, if your husband asked you to kill your son, you would not submit to his request. Perhaps he asks you to lie, cheat, or steal. In any of those cases, your allegiance to the Lord would forbid you from submitting to your husband. Having a sound hermeneutic is critical when interpreting Bible words, verses, passages, meanings, and contexts.

A wife is to submit to her husband, and she should be humble and respectful toward her husband, but as I have told my wife many times, if she does not share what she thinks, she is not serving me effectively or honoring God completely. I do not want a doormat wife. I do not want her to agree with me just because it may be the path of least resistance. I want a wife who can boldly appeal but yet humbly submit to me. I want a wife who can think for herself. Of course, it's incumbent upon me to create a context of grace where she experiences the freedom to speak her mind according to how she is hearing from God. I need my wife to complement me (Genesis 2:18). We need each other.

- Husband, how have you created a context of grace in your home that motivates your wife to share her authentic thoughts?
- How do you hinder her from being free within the marriage to share openly, honestly, and transparently?
- Wife, are you willing to step up courageously and serve your husband and honor God by appealing to

him according to how God is leading you?
- Do you respect your husband?

It's Not About the Decision

When decisions divide, there is something wrong with the marriage. The marriage is a one-flesh union that nothing divides except death, which is why decision-making is a beautiful opportunity to assess your relationship with each other. Decisions are opportunities to put Christ on display in your marriage. Suppose you do not make Christ your centerpiece because of childishness, fighting, and pettiness. In that case, the decision you're attempting to make becomes a mirror that shows the condition of your relationship. If your marriage cannot withstand the decision-making process or the outcome of the decisions that you make, you need to find help because there is something wrong. There is nothing that should continuously disrupt the unity and harmony found in the marriage union. The husband and wife are a picture of Christ and His church (Ephesians 5:21–33).

- What does your decision-making process typically reveal about your marriage?
- Are you a cohesive team, a divided couple, or somewhere in the middle?
- Do you look forward to tackling problems together?
- What do you need to change to become better partners in the decision-making process?

The Gospel Drives Decision-Making

A couple who rightly understands the gospel realizes that Christ resolved their biggest problem at the cross. There is nothing they will ever face that will come close to the problem they had at Adam's tree. Because of this gospel reality, a couple interacts with each other as grateful friends who see all of life as a gift. This couple is not controlled by what they get or do not get because they live in the daily awareness of doing far better than they deserve. Their pressing desires do not dictate or drive them. They live in the daily contentment that Christ offers through the gospel. Gratitude characterizes them.

It is no longer about wins or losses. Their ambitions are for the glory of God, not for personal gain or glory-robbing. They will accept a "no" just as easily as they accept a "yes." It's not about either one but about accomplishing God's will in their relationship. There is no tug-of-war between them, but two people are pulling in the same direction. They are mutually cheering for each other while living in the daily amazement of the gospel. They seek the interest of the other (Matthew 22:36–40).

> *Do nothing from rivalry or conceit, but in humility count others more significant than yourselves. Let each of you look not only to his own interests, but also to the interests of others.*
> *(Philippians 2:3–4)*

- How does the gospel affect your spouse in the decision-making process?
- How does it affect you?
- Do you have to win, regardless of the outcome? Why or why not?
- Are you genuinely seeking to accept your spouse's position?
- Is your first instinct to find the good in your spouse's point of view?

Call to Action

I have given you more than two dozen questions to ponder and practicalize. Let these questions be your marital homework assignment over the next couple of weeks. You could go on a few life over coffee dates to discuss what you've just read.

Making Decisions as a Couple

5

May I Change My Mind?

You have made your decision in faith. At the time, it seemed like the right thing to do. Now you're having second thoughts. Is it okay to change your mind? Or are you bound to the decision you have made with no other alternative but to live with the consequences? Is it possible to be in faith for the decision, but things have changed to such a degree that you have the biblical right to change your mind?

Even biblical decision-making is an imperfect process because all of us are subjective. Only God can look at a situation and make an objective decision. We're always working from a fallen condition that is not sanctified entirely. Plus, due to our lack of omniscience, we're operating with limited data. Thus, it's not unusual to make a decision and then have buyer's remorse. I'm sure that after Peter decided to get off the boat and walk to Jesus, he doubted his decision (Matthew 14:28–33). There are times when the Lord orchestrates adverse outcomes from our decisions and we should not seek another path forward (2 Corinthians 1:8–9). At other times, we make a poor decision, and God's wisdom suggests we do something different. However, before you change your mind about something that you thought was the right thing to do, make sure you assess yourself properly.

Five Assessments

- **BE TEACHABLE:** Humility is a gift from God (James 4:6). Ask God for this mercy and pursue it aggressively. It is the best gift when making a decision. Coming to the Father with a "not my will, but Your will be done" attitude is the way you want to begin the process of making a decision or rethinking a past decision.
- **BE SUSPICIOUS:** If you understand that the log is in your eye (Matthew 7:3-5), you will be humbly suspicious of yourself. It is wisdom and humility to consider that you could be wrong in a matter. Suspicion does not have to be fear-based, but it must be discernment-based. We are self-deceived in certain areas. We have blind spots. We are in the wrong place if we think we have all the right answers. Healthy suspicion is a good thing.
- **PRAY OFTEN:** Talking to God should go without saying, but I will say it anyway. Spend much time with your Father, seeking and asking while expressing gratitude for His continued acceptance of you and favor in your life. Pray much (1 Thessalonians 5:16-18).
- **SEARCH THE SCRIPTURES:** The Bible will give you direct and indirect commands. Scriptures will tell you directly not to commit adultery, not to steal, and not to get drunk. It will say to serve others, to forgive others, and to be kind to others. The Bible is clear in many ways. However, the Bible does not speak specifically to every situation, like whether you should go to college or start a Roth IRA. You can apply some Scriptures to your life directly. There

are other things where you want to move cautiously. Either way, the Bible gives you all you need for life and godliness. See 2 Peter 1:3.
- **SEEK COUNSEL:** You will find wisdom and safety in counsel (Proverbs 24:6). Seek those who are a little farther down the road than you are. Though I'm not opposed to peer counseling, I would caution anyone about receiving counsel from those who are similar to you. Find the individuals you trust and who possess the wisdom to speak to your situation.

With these assessments in view, how would you rate yourself? Meeting with a friend to do life over coffee would be perfect for evaluating yourself. Here are your questions.

- Are you a teachable person?
- Are you appropriately suspicious of yourself?
- Have you been praying often about this matter?
- Do you know what God's Word says about your decision?
- Is the person helping you make your decision competent?

Even abiding by the best methods found in the Bible, it is possible to make a decision that you regret. Perhaps it was the wrong decision. Maybe it was the right thing to do, but you're struggling with doubt. Fortunately, the solution is not that complicated. Here are two guiding truths that can help when it comes to second-guessing your decisions.

Maintain a Biblical Course

It's okay to change your mind as long as your new decision is biblically better and biblically permitted. Perhaps new information that you didn't have came to light after you made the initial decision. Here are three examples of this idea.

Example #1:
You change your mind about being married.

To get married is a biblical, God-honoring decision, but there are three ways in which you can change your mind about being married. Death is the one change that you have no control over; it happens, and you have to change your mind when death comes. The other two options that allow you to change your mind are abandonment and adultery, as spelled out in 1 Corinthians 7 and Matthew 19. These three conditions permit you to change your mind about being married. However, it's important to know that biblical permission to leave your marriage—according to options two and three—does not mean you should leave your marriage. Though Matthew 19 and 1 Corinthians 7 are part of God's infallible Word, the greater point of God's entire Word is reconciliation. From Genesis to Revelation, the purpose of God's Word is God reconciling Himself to humanity. Just because you may have an out, it does not mean you have to take it, though, under these three stipulations outlined in God's Word, you can change your mind about your marriage.

Example #2:
You can change your mind if you are in sin.

If you choose to commit adultery, for instance, changing your mind is not only preferable but mandated. In such a case, you decided to sin, and at some point afterward, you came to another decision. You have new information, and you believe it is better than the past information—the choice to sin. In such a case, you change your mind and begin living according to the new information. This change of mind is also called repentance.

Example #3: You can change your mind if there is new or better information.

You make all kinds of decisions throughout your life. You base these decisions on the information you possess at the time. Later, based on new data or different circumstances, you decide that another course of action is the best route to take. Maybe you have received better counsel. Perhaps there is new information, and now you have come to a different awareness. It may not have been a sin to make the first decision, as opposed to example #2, but now you realize it would be better to change your mind. In such cases, it is not wrong. Though you were in faith before, you are no longer in faith to stay in the same place. You change your mind and move in a different direction with a new belief.

Understand Progressive Sanctification

Changing your mind happens all the time with progressive sanctification (1 Corinthians 13:11). There are many things that I believed were right when God first regenerated me, but I have come to a different place in my faith. I've changed my mind about the type of Bible I read, the clothes I wear, the music I listen to, and the places I go. There are many more areas where I have changed my mind, and I hope to continue to change my mind on many things throughout my life. If you want to mature as a Christian, you must change your mind in ways that are biblically better and biblically permitted.

Call to Action

1. What is your motive for changing your mind?
2. Does the Bible permit you to change your mind about an issue?
3. Are you sinning to change your mind to a new way of living?
4. If you do change your mind, what new information (or situation) has come to light?
5. What do the Canon, community, and Comforter say about you changing your mind?

6

Torment Is Perfection

Have you ever tried to be perfect? Is it hard for you to let others know you messed up? Are you tempted to present yourself in ways that are not exactly true to who you are? Maybe when you think about others learning the real truth about you, it strikes momentary fear in your heart. Suppose your spouse brought a friend home unannounced. Does it matter what your home looks like at that moment?

Perfectionism's Struggle

If you answered yes to my questions, you might struggle with perfectionism. Here is a more important question: Can you embrace the Bible's testimony that you are imperfect and all that being imperfect implies? Striving to be perfect is a problem, but what makes it worse is that it's not an isolated issue. Like all our sin problems, the perfectionist collects other bad habits that attach themselves to this core heart problem. Here are six possibilities.

- **A FORM OF LYING:** Whenever a person tries to be something they are not, deceit is happening. The so-called perfectionist is not real with himself or with other people that he wants to impress.

- **WORSHIP DYSFUNCTION:** Rather than finding his identity in Christ's perfection, he hopes others will accept him for his accomplishments. Financial status, well-performing children, and a good reputation are some of the self-worship idols he erects.
- **SELF-DECEPTION:** As he continues down this unattainable path, his thinking begins to harden his conscience, which creates a separation between where he is and the power of the cross that could change him. Any sin held onto will deaden the conscience.
- **LACK OF INTEGRITY:** His character becomes tarnished by his unsavory loyalty to himself. Nobody could trust him ultimately because of his willingness to deceive people, even though it might not be an overt intention to be deceptive.
- **INSECURITY:** The perfectionist will always be insecure around those he wants to gain acceptance. He is only secure when the individuals he wants to please accept him. A person like this will have ongoing frustration and disappointment in his life.
- **SECRET SINS:** One of the side-effects of striving perfectionists is the need to find relief from the stress of the pursuit of perfectionism. It is not unusual for them to find pseudo-alleviation through secret lusts like sexual problems, overeating, or anger patterns.

What Does It Mean?

The so-called perfectionist is a slave to an illusionary idea. He may be a believer, but he does not know what full freedom in Christ means experientially. He will always fall short of perfectionism as well as the freedom that Christ has called him to enjoy. The bottom line for the wannabe perfectionist is his unwillingness to trust God. His striving for perfection is a loud commentary on how he thinks about God. Rather than finding acceptance (and rest) through the finished work of Christ, he continues to strive for the perfection that only Christ can deliver. This tension puts him in a tug-of-war with God. It is as though the Lord is saying,

> I fully forgive you for all of your past, present, and future sins. I give you my Son's perfect righteousness. I do not see you as a sinner but as a righteous child. Please enter into my rest.

The perfectionist says,

> I affirm in my mind what you are saying, but it is still important that others think a certain way about me. To satisfy this craving, I have to control certain situations. I cannot let them know the real me, which is why I try to perpetuate a slightly altered image.

Solution

The perfectionist needs to repent, but that creates a problem. For him to repent, he will have to let others know that he is not perfect. He will have to let some of his friends in on the charade. Being transparent and honest is nearly impossible for a proud perfectionist.

Path Forward

If you struggle with perfectionistic tendencies, find someone you trust and who is competent enough to walk you through this problem. You will have to spill the beans. You've got to let someone know you are a sinner-in-hiding. Transparency will be hard for you because you crave their approval and fear anything that smacks of criticism. In addition, you must come to terms with the gospel. The gospel means many things, but there is one thing for certain: you are perfectly perfect in Christ. There is not one iota of any amount of work that you can do to make yourself more acceptable to God. The truths of the gospel must be your truths—practically speaking. You must own them today and every day from this point forward while repenting of this illusionary notion that you need the approval of others.

A NOTE FOR THOSE WORKING WITH PERFECTIONISTS: You must humbly love, care for, and serve them because they are in bondage to the gods of approval, respect, honor, significance, and acceptance. You must know and understand their sinful tendencies and be able to come alongside them in a non-condemnatory way. They do not fully trust God (or you) at this point. I'm not necessarily speaking of their regeneration but their post-salvation experience with God, also called progressive sanctification. They need to lean on your faith as you carefully and gently show them the way to God.

Prayer

Dear Father,

I am not perfect, and I can never be perfect. I need a perfect Savior. I have been born again by the power of the gospel. I am regenerated. Today, I am adopted by and positioned in Christ. When you see me, you see your Son in me. Father, I pray you will break the bondage that has trapped my soul. It haunts me and teaches me that I need to perform for others to be accepted by them. I can never adequately serve others if I live as though I need them. I want to serve them properly, not be controlled by my perception of their opinions of me.

Though I am not an overt hypocrite, there are certain individuals and situations where I want to impress or be impressive. When I do this, I obscure the work of the Savior in me. Help me to rest in this singular truth: I am perfect in Him, and I do not need to perform for others. Make this prayer practically real to me, Father. Change me from the inside out. Transform me by the power of the gospel. May that which saved me also sanctify me. Help me to be satisfied with you alone.

Thank you.

Amen

Call to Action

Will you talk to a friend about any perfectionistic struggles you may have? Perhaps sharing this chapter will help both of you enter into a heart-transforming, friendship-deepening discussion.

Case Studies

7

The Double Minded

Every person has two heads. The human community is a world of two-headed people. James called our common-to-man predicament double-mindedness, just one of the characteristics that comes with our Adamic packaging. At times, we think and act one way, and at other times, we think and act like a different person. If you find yourself occasionally oscillating between two or more personalities and unable to find your true north, you're normal.

Lacking Wisdom

> If any of you lacks wisdom, let him ask God, who gives generously to all without reproach, and it will be given him. But let him ask in faith, with no doubting, for the one who doubts is like a wave of the sea that is driven and tossed by the wind. For that person must not suppose that he will receive anything from the Lord; he is a double-minded man, unstable in all his ways.
>
> (James 1:5–6)

James understood human psychology—the study of the soul—and was not surprised when he observed odd behavior from his friends. Of course, being Jesus's half-brother had to be a plus in his ongoing discipleship training and relationship-making. Moving back and forth from faith to fear and back to faith again is our mutual human experience. Some days, we stand on the promises of God and other days, we feel buried under an avalanche of other things that disrupt our faith. We can be like the father with the sick boy in Mark 9:24: "Lord, I believe. Help my unbelief." To varying degrees, we will be unbelieving believers until Jesus returns. Perfect, uninterrupted faith is a great idea, but it is impossible for fallen people because of impure hearts and sin's encroachments.

Impure hearts represent the hidden things that need the clarity of God's Word to bring to the surface (Hebrews 4:13). Part of fear's deception motivates us to hide behind our fig leaves (Genesis 3:7). We are afraid, which prompts us to keep these things from others. If we don't have unhindered access to our friends, there will be times when their actions will appear unstable. Their behavior will confuse us when they begin acting in strange ways. There are two conditions contribute that create this kind of behavior.

- Your friend has not been open about their life because they are afraid to be transparent with you.
- You have not been intrusive enough because you do not understand this aspect of human psychology, or you do not care enough—for whatever reason—to dig deeper into their lives.

James instructs us about the possibilities of another life that exists inside of us—a manifestation of a fear-based person—and what can happen when fear controls our hearts. This problem is why our behavior moves so easily from stability to instability. Let me illustrate with a case study.

YOU DECIDE

The Churning Soul

Mable married Biff twenty-one years ago. For most of those years, Biff has had an anger problem. He has a selfish ideal of how life should be, and when it does not go according to his gospel, he reacts with anger. Sometimes, Biff was volatile and accusative. Other times, he would sulk like Ahab, manipulating the situation through silence (1 Kings 21:5). He has trained Mable well. She learned the ropes early, knowing when to speak and when not to speak. Biff has been mostly unaware of what has been going on in Mable's heart. From his perspective, she was fine as long as she was not demanding too much from him. What he did not perceive was that Mable was building a secret world in her heart that was wrapped in fear.

Initially, Mable's secret world was mostly about being afraid of Biff. But as the marriage progressed and his anger continued unabated, her fear metastasized into bitterness, frustration, hopelessness, unforgiveness, regret, jealousy, and hurt. These were soul-diminishing combinations for Mable, who had no avenues to find help. She lost herself in women's ministry, but ministry is not a sanctification solution for a troubled marriage. Ignoring a problem by working harder for the Lord does not work. A prison of silence had incarcerated Mable, and it was churning in her soul. Then, with seemingly no provocation and to Biff's complete surprise, she went off the deep end, exploding at Biff just before she walked out the door for the last time.

The Unexplored Wife

Biff sat in my office dumbfounded. From his perspective, the marriage was good, though not fabulous. He worked hard. He provided for his family. They lived in the best neighborhood and lacked virtually nothing. He was genuinely perplexed by her behavior. He was even more overwhelmed by her emails that laid out what seemed to be everything she had thought but never said for the past two decades. Biff said,

> I have no idea who this woman is. It's like she has two heads. We have been married for more than twenty years, and now I believe that I have married a stranger.

He is right. He does not know Mable.

He has made little effort to understand her beyond getting a handle on the misguided love language teaching. He gave her what she wanted but could not provide what she needed. His attempts to care for his wife never went beyond behavioral modification or his commitment to do better, which always ran out of gas. He understood her as much as he wanted to, and if there were things that would challenge his obligation to do soul care, he would not delve deeper with Mable. Biff liked his wife, but being caught in his sin of anger, coupled with her double-minded fear, things were more complicated than they should have been for their marriage to survive. Their relationship gives a more profound and nuanced meaning to Peter's appeal:

> Likewise, husbands, live with your wives in an understanding way, showing honor to the woman as the weaker vessel, since they are heirs with you of the grace of life, so that your prayers may not be hindered.
>
> (1 Peter 3:7)

Living Oscillators

Warning:

This case study is a theological and psychological study about how fear morphs into other sin patterns that perpetuate dysfunction in relationships. It is not a discussion about blame, especially placing primary responsibility on Mable for the demise of their marriage. The point of this chapter is to help identify what happens in our hearts if we don't bring our fears into the light and proper soul care happens. James suggests that we all have the propensity not to trust God fully. He says when doubt comes, our behavior will move toward instability. This problem is the human condition that Adam and Eve gifted to us (Romans 5:12) and the primary point I'm addressing here, though there is much to say about Biff, the initiator and primary culprit in this marriage case study.

Mable was not entirely sanctified, and Biff's anger exposed her hidden fears. Their lives were a silent and vicious cycle. Biff would bark, and Mable would melt. Mable was much more aware of what was happening to her, but she was obviously afraid to confront her husband. She was lost somewhere between faith and fear, with no one to care for her. Biff was mostly oblivious and unqualified, and her community did not know what was happening inside their home. Biff had the opportunity and privilege to understand his wife, but he not only fell on the job, he complicated an already complicated soul. He rolled through his home large and in charge, and Mable learned to toe the line, trying to keep him happy while silently longing for Biff to love her well. There was only so much silence her soul could contain before it overflowed into shocking behavior.

Tips For the Double Mind

Because Mable is an illustration of all of us, here are two things to think about when you are tempted to go into two-headedness.

YOU CANNOT LIVE LIKE THIS: It is impossible to live in an ongoing suspension between fear and faith without it negatively affecting your soul. Mable is a typical example of a person stuck in this tension. There was a truth she perceived about her life and marriage, but she was not correctly appropriating the grace the Lord provides. Mable was understandably afraid of her husband, but she was unwittingly pressing the truth she knew further down into her soul (James 4:17). Paul talked about this in Romans.

> For the wrath of God is revealed from heaven against all ungodliness and unrighteousness of men, who by their unrighteousness suppress the truth.
> (Romans 1:18)

This verse sounds harsh when applied to someone like Mable, who is a victim of her husband's anger. I do not mean it harshly, but theologically. Carefully unpack what Paul is saying. The Lord is in opposition to anyone who will not reach out for His truth in their time of need but chooses to suppress the truth while doing things their way. If you humble yourself and trust His way through the process, He will provide a path forward. If you do not follow His way through the process, He will be the opposition (James 4:6).

If you are in need of God's wisdom, do not suppress it out of your life by not seeking it while clinging to your way of fixing your problems. That approach will lead to death (Proverbs 14:12, 16:25). Mable was doing what James said not to do, and she was experiencing a slow death by a thousand paper cuts. It first began as fear. Rather than seeking the Lord's wisdom, she suppressed her fear. What she did not know was how her fear was going to metastasize. As the years went by, a host of other sins began to attach themselves to her soul. In time, this became more than she could endure. Even in the end, she did not seek the Lord's wisdom but chose to leave her marriage.

You Must Get Help: James says if you lack wisdom, you must ask for it, bringing us to a crucial question: how do you find wisdom? Some individuals teach that all you have to do is pray. That singular act will not work well because the Lord's wisdom comes to us in various ways. Prayer is essential, no doubt. Then there is the Word of God. We also have the illuminating power of the Spirit of God. Lastly, we have the community of God. The Lord has placed countermeasures with checks and balances to ensure we have His pure wisdom that comes from above. This multi-perspective approach keeps us from engaging in foolish behavior.

- If you act on your own, there will be temptations of self-deception and self-reliance.
- If you are Spirit-centered without the counterbalance of God's Word and God's people, you may fall into subjectivism.
- If you only use God's Word, you may misunderstand and misapply it.
- If you access the community of faith alone, the advice may not be Spirit-illuminated or Bible-based.

Call to Action

The wisdom of the Lord is needful, but we must access it in a comprehensive fashion. Mable did not do this. She should have responded to Biff with love, grace, and courage. Though God calls her to submit to her husband, she has every right to confront him. As things were, Mable did not love her husband biblically. Sin had caught Biff in a trap (cf. Galatians 6:1–2) and she could have been a major means of grace to restore him in a spirit of gentleness. Though she is not responsible for his sin, and there are many other angles to their marriage problems, for this case study, we're focusing on Mable's double-mindedness and how she got there. With this in view, here are six tips that will help anyone in a similar place.

1. You must determine that you're going to seek the wisdom of the Lord.
2. You must use all the means of grace available to you to keep you centered in God's wisdom.
3. You must attempt to speak with your spouse, letting them know what is happening to you. (The assumption is your spouse is mature enough to handle what you need to say. If your spouse is not, you must find help outside of your marriage.)
4. You must ensure that you're in a safe context where you can share what is going on in your heart, revealing your innermost thoughts.
5. If your spouse refuses to get help, you must continue to trust the Lord by seeking wisdom from others on how to navigate your marriage.
6. You must find ongoing care because the temptation to oscillate between fear and faith will be strong.

Like Aaron and Hur holding up the arms of Moses, you will need support from competent friends (Exodus 17:12). You cannot go back into the prison of your marriage without help because you will default to the habituation of fear and all its accompanying and unwanted enemies of the soul. As you continue to trust the Lord by fighting for your soul and your marriage, you may need to access the protective and authoritative care of your local church. If your relationship regresses, the church must become your covering and voice.

8

Married the Wrong Person

It is easy to make a decision when things seem clear and the future appears bright. With an optimistic heart, you decide on that thing, only to discover months or years later that it may not be wise to do what you did. What if that decision was to marry someone that you now believe was the wrong person? Sometimes, you cannot redo what you believe is a wrong decision. What are you supposed to do now?

Marriage Gone Awry

In chapter two, I ask what the most critical question you can ask when making a decision is. The answer is, "Are you in faith to move forward with your decision?" Many times in my counseling career, folks have come to me questioning whether they made the right decision when they got married. They thought they were in love, believed it was the right thing to do, and were in faith, so they got married. But things have gone awry, and their faith for the marriage is now languishing.

At other times, there have been situations where two people were married, but they did not have the best motives for getting married. Now, fifteen years later, they are convinced they made a wrong decision on their wedding day, so the dissatisfied couple is asking why they should stay married. The first couple did not know all that they wished they had known, and the other couple knew better but chose not to respond the right way to what they sensed in their spirit. These dilemmas are more common than you might imagine. Typically, when you fully unpack the above scenarios, two primary issues come into view.

- A Truncated View of the Sovereignty of God
- A Selfish Desire to Escape God's Work in Your Life

Truncated View of Sovereignty

There is no way to know God's will with absolute certainty when you look into the future. God does not give us all of the future information we want about our lives. James 4:13-15 teaches us to say that "if it is the Lord's will, we shall do this or that." Therefore, the best we can do is move forward by faith. Would you prefer to place your faith in having all the details laid out before you? Or would you rather place your faith in the Lord, knowing that He knows the beginning from the end and that He will take care of you? (See Philippians 1:6.)

Where you land on those questions will determine how you respond when the going gets tough. It is not unusual to get into a future situation only to find out later that the circumstances have taken a turn for the worse (Matthew 14:30). In fact, you can guarantee that part of your future will be disappointing (2 Corinthians 4:7-10). The story of Joseph in the Old Testament is a sober reminder of a person who experienced a future strewn with difficulty. But Joseph had enough sovereign clarity to understand the mysteries of God, knowing the Lord was working a plan for the good of many (Genesis 50:20). His faith was in God rather than knowing all the details of the outcome. In some marriage situations, the relationship has gone wrong, though the person thought it was a good idea in the beginning. In other cases, there is the person who was never in true faith to get married but did it anyway and is now contemplating ending the marriage. In either case, God speaks to these them in two clear ways.

OPTION #1: Ultimately, you cannot do anything outside of God's decreed will. God could stop you if He wanted to do so. We may make our plans, but God is the one who orders our steps (Proverbs 16:9). If He permits your steps, even though they take you to some difficult places, the Lord will be there before you arrive (Exodus 1:5). Even when we mess up, the glory of God will shine through our finite and imperfect planning. Most certainly, our lives are not all about us. God can use sin sinlessly, and even though your choice to marry may not have been the best decision, God still guides, either by allowing, hindering, or stopping the covenant. Since He did not stop your covenant relationship with your spouse and you are married, now it's time for you to trust Him and His purposes for your life rather than seeking to end what He has permitted.

OPTION #2: God only gives three clear ways to end a marriage: death, adultery, and abandonment. These sad circumstances do not mean that you should dissolve your union, even though in the case of adultery or desertion, it is a biblical option. (See Matthew 19 and 1 Corinthians 7.) Let your next decision be to trust God. Rest in Him. He is perfectly working even when you are not correctly applying. Whether you had the right faith or no faith in your marriage, it is not a biblical option for you to end your marriage. He is calling you to trust Him now, even though you may not have done that as well as you could have when you married.

Desire to Escape God's Work

Somebody, somehow, and at some level, is being selfish in the marriage. It is always both spouses, though one can be more selfish than the other. If the desire to get married were selfish, it would not be a surprise that the motive for divorce is (to some degree) selfish as well. A better approach would be to work on the issues related to selfishness rather than look for an escape clause to get out of the marriage. Doing things the way you want to do them may be the reason you're married, but you don't want to make that mistake a second time by doing what you want to because things are hard for you.

If your motives are not entirely pure at this point, divorce will not rectify the real problem. My recommendation would be to get some help for yourself and fight for your marriage. Your wisdom may be finite, and you're not entirely comfortable with where you are in your covenant or who you have married, but let me urge you to rest in the One who is not finite, and He can lead better than anyone else. Though it may seem this marriage was meant for evil, I can tell you that God means it for good. Honor your covenant. It will take some work to get there, but it is worth it. Be sure to find competent, biblical help because you're too subjective now. You need people who are outside of your marriage to help you practically.

YOU DECIDE

Call to Action

1. What does it mean for you to honor your covenant?
2. Have you ever wondered if you had married the right person? Have you worked through the doubt? If not, what is your plan to be at peace with God and your spouse?
3. How would you counsel someone who believed they had married the wrong person?
4. Discuss with a friend how a truncated view of the sovereignty of God has affected your life.
5. Discuss with a friend about how your motives were not pure when you made a decision, but you see God's hand in it anyway.

Married the Wrong Person

9

Get the Vaccine Already

The whole world was at war in 2020. It was a war between good and evil. We understand skirmishes were between military combatants, but the purpose of this chapter is not between those warriors in the traditional theaters. I'm addressing those other warriors—those who might not have been to war but live in a fallen world where the evil one roams about, seeking to devour us. I'm speaking to you and me. We have an adversary; he is the devil. The irony of our modern-day war is that it came to us in the most innocuous of ways: should you take the vaccine or not?

Purposeful Freedom

Disclosure: Our family chose not to get vaccinated. Perhaps like you, we have less trust in faceless entities who do not know me, do not have my best interest in view, and care more about their agendas or personal successes than my life.

I do not sense the need to compete or begrudge an individual's ambitions or life goals, but when their objectives require my adherence to help them reach their life goals, I tend to resist full submission to their talking points. When public servants lose their call to serve, I distance myself from their practices and policies, using other criteria for determining if I want to follow their warnings or consequences. However, because the Bible does not prohibit or mandate a vaccine, our posture must be purposeful freedom. This perspective means that each person has to choose based on criteria that are unique to them. It does not have to be a sin to get the vaccine, and it does not have to be wrong to refrain from it. To his own master, a person will stand or fall. Thus, as with all decisions, you choose your master and stand or fall accordingly.

Overall Beliefs

Without being a cynic, my discernment guides me from going all in with folks who promote themselves to being on the right side of things when there are many other policymakers and good people who are against what is rousing my suspicions. For example, many of those who wanted me to get a vaccine reject my God. If they are wrong about God, could they be wrong in their utopian view of life? I'm not suggesting every unbeliever is wrong about everything or that every believer is always right. There are many unbelievers I love to read, listen to, and learn from, and there is a growing list of believers that I do not trust.

To expect no wolves with the sheep or no weeds among the flowers is a naive way to live one's life. I'm reasonably comfortable with weeds and wolves, but everyone named Red Riding Hood is not my friend. I recognize that many believers believe in the vaccine, and they would suggest that I'm wrong on this matter. I can accept their view as long as they don't make their preference my mandate. Once dogmatism becomes the order over Christian charity (among believers), I have to question the sincerity of the dogma and the dogmatist. If we cannot agree to disagree over secondary issues, then those who won't permit Christian charity create a red flag that is hard for me to unsee.

Anti-Science

I was listening to a lady with a daughter who was adversely affected by the vaccine. She stated that she was pro-science, which sounded (sort of) like an apology. I doubt she intended how it sounded on the video, but she suggested that she was pro-science, but [this] happened. I've heard this apologetic before; when some folks talk science, it sounds like if you don't believe the current scientific narrative, you're anti-science. It begs the question: you can be pro-science and not take the vaccine. Can't you? Again, when a scientific position has only one option with no dissent, I struggle with the scientific position.

I've lived long enough to follow the science, only realizing later that it's unwise to follow that science any longer. If any person had followed science from 2020 to 2023, you'd see how science has repeatedly jumped from one antithesis to another. When politicians and pundits refuse to be honest about these vacillations, they do not instill confidence among the masses. You can be pro-science and have a wait-and-see posture to let the science prove itself. As such, the back and forth with the science does not create confidence but undercuts the points the authoritarians want to mandate.

Contradictory Science

One of the odder components of this controversy is not allowing the science to stand on its merit. For example, if the vaccines work, then any person who gets a vaccine should be fine—if the science is true, and it would not matter what choices others make. Each person must choose how risk-averse they want to be, and if someone is not risk-averse to forego the vaccine, they have the right to become vaccinated. Let me illustrate:

- **FLU ILLUSTRATION:** In years past, each individual or family would make the flu shot decision, which was not a matter of public policy or debate. If you got it, you assumed reasonable protection from the strain of flu. If you chose not to get it, you accepted the risks.
- **ALCOHOL ILLUSTRATION:** If I don't want to become an alcoholic, I must not drink alcohol (or, at least, moderate), but it's not enough for me to not drink, but you must not drink as well, as though your choice to drink will make me a person with an addiction. Some will argue it's apples and oranges, which is not the case if the vaccine's efficacy is sure and steadfast.

The Metanarrative

The vaccine—apparently—is a Trojan Horse to a more complex issue, as more data comes from China. We know that part of the Chinese government's philosophy for world dominance is to plant a thousand flowers to see which ones will grow. (Perhaps Kudzu would be a better analogy.) China has not been secretive about its aspiration for world dominance, and one of its more successful initiatives has been its gain-of-function research and implementation of a global pandemic. What Is gain of function? Illustration—A person takes a rock and adds a function to it to make it a brick. Now, it's more potent than a rock. Then he adds another function to make it a cement block; it has gained a function. Later, he added another component to make it a boulder; it continues to gain more functionality. Lastly, he adds one more function until it's an avalanche. If you keep adding new functions to a virus, eventually, you can have a super-virus that brings the world to its knees.

There are also those in America who do the bidding of those who hate our country. Some of these folks are co-conspirators or, perhaps, ignorant. Their greed has created myopia that blinds them to our country's autoimmune disease, which is eating away at its constitutional core. Disney, LeBron James, and Apple Corporation are three of these conspirators. We must not divorce ourselves from this metanarrative (grand narrative) while we make daily decisions about whether to vax or not to vax. It's the daily decisions to stand for personal freedom that will bring the fight to those who want to roll their agenda over you. Too many of us discount our lives and micro-decisions as though our tiny drops of water in the ocean do not affect the sea. Perhaps that is correct with one droplet, but when millions of folks make the same non-combative, non-resistant decision, it becomes collective guilt and blame.

The Least Path

Most Christians continue to kick the can of conflict and confrontation down the road. They don't want to make the hard decisions. They procrastinate while silently cheering those in the public eye who hold their views. This posture is no longer tenable. Glomming personal cowardice on the courage of others is anti-Christian. The person who knows the right thing to do and chooses not to do it is a sinning, procrastinating individual (James 4:17). The proven path to least resistance leads to a cross, not some other ideal. The person who avoids the cross will find their souls bleeding out in a Potter's Field. There is a way that seems right to the carnal mind, but it will prove—over and over again—to be the path to an inglorious death that adds no value to God's fame or the salvation of souls.

It has now become atrocious to spend our days on social media, sharing our favorite quote from our favorite hero, hoping it will be enough to turn the tide. Wormwood could not be more pleased. Without being mean toward others, we can no longer self-censor. We can be full of grace and truth, but it must be more than that. There are other costs to count, the first of which will be our courage—or the lack thereof. Teddy Roosevelt got it right in this over-used but most relevant quote.

> It is not the critic who counts; not the man who points out how the strong man stumbles, or where the doer of deeds could have done them better. The credit belongs to the man who is actually in the arena, whose face is marred by dust and sweat and blood; who strives valiantly; who errs, who comes short again and again, because there is no effort without error and shortcoming; but who does actually strive to do the deeds; who knows great enthusiasms, the great devotions; who spends himself in a worthy cause; who at the best knows in the end the triumph of high achievement, and who at the worst, if he fails, at least fails while daring greatly, so that his place shall never be with those cold and timid souls who neither know victory nor defeat. - Theodore Roosevelt

Count the Cost

I do not know if you should get a vaccine. I would not impose my view on you because the Bible does not specifically tell us what to do about this matter, which brings us back to purposeful freedom. But what I do know is that we cannot take the role of a spectator. We must activate our faith, which is the only kind of faith there is. We must make many decisions and then reacquaint ourselves with them each day, adjusting what we must and marching forth as ambassadors of Christ, courageous regardless of the cost. The cost will be more than taking or refusing the vaccine. We may have to leave our churches, break away from relatives, move from our communities, find other jobs, or suffer incarceration. I'm not an alarmist, though what I'm suggesting may sound alarming to those who have never given up much for the cause of Christ.

Most Christians have a standard of living, and it's that standard that means more to them than whatever insidiousness that is eating away at their freedoms. The silent cancer is no longer silent. If you don't see these things, ask the Lord to provide you with eyes to see them. If you're unwilling to look, ask the Lord to grant repentance so you can unbury your head from the malaise. The community of Christ must come together in a spirit of love and boldness that penetrates our dark world for the fame of God, the cause of Christ, and the redemption of many hopeless souls.

Call to Action

1. Should you get the vaccine? If "yes," state your case. If "no," state your case. How do you support your view with God's Word?
2. **COMMUNITY:** What trusted friend have you discussed this issue with? What is their view? How have you agreed, agreed to disagree, and remained friends?
3. **CONSCIENCE:** Your conscience is your inner voice; it is your highest level of moral authority; you must not sin against your conscience. Is your conscience in tune with God's Word? If it is not, what must you do to bring your conscience in line with God's Word?
4. **COMFORTER:** Are there any ways you are quenching or grieving the Spirit of God? If there are any, what are your specific plans to change so the Spirit and you are singing the same song?
5. **CANON:** Defend your position with God's Word. If you cannot do this, find someone to help you walk through how to do it. Do not be careless. Be honest with your Bible knowledge and test your

assumptions. Christians have nothing to hide, protect, or fear. If you have things to hide, protect, or fear, you must address these matters because to be free.

6. **Costs:** What are the costs of your decision? As you decide, what are your plans to be a redemptive force in your church and community? Be specific.

Conclusion

If you could live your life over again, how would you live it differently? What values would you instill to give yourself a meaningful life? What if you could instill those values now? An excellent way to think about these things is to ask someone—people farther down wisdom's road than you are.

Survey Says

Years ago, someone told me about a study of older adults. The question asked was, "If they could live their life over again, what would they do differently?" I was so impressed by their answers that they became a template for how I wanted to live my life. Here are their top three responses:

- I would take more risks.
- I would do important things.
- I would spend more time reflecting.

I took their responses, ran them through a biblical grid, and came up with the following life plan:

- I will step out in biblical faith as often as possible.
- I will do things that impact lives for generations.
- I will spend time in meditative, reflective thought.

Conclusion

Taking Risks

Taking risks without biblical guidance could be the errand of a fool. Taking biblical risks is godly. Christians are not passive or impulsive. Christians are intentional and informed risk-takers. It reminds me of Peter, who was standing on a boat during a dark and stormy night (Matthew 14:28–33). Christ was asking him to take a biblical risk. Peter was nervous about the offer for obvious reasons. Who walks on water? Peter was willing, but he needed assurance. Thus, he asked, "Is that you, Lord?" An important question. Christian decisions are faith-informed decisions. Once you inform your faith through the means of grace the Lord provides, nothing is left to do but get off the boat. There are the four means of grace for faith-informed decisions.

- **CANON:** What does God's Word say about what you want to do?
- **COMFORTER:** How is the Spirit of God illuminating your mind about what you want to do?
- **COMMUNITY:** What do your close, competent, courageous Christian friends say about what you want to do?
- **CONSCIENCE:** How is your "inner voice" speaking to you about what you want to do?

RISK QUESTION: What is God asking you to do but you're afraid to do it? You don't want to come to the end of your life with a boatload of "would've, should've, could've" regrets.

Eternal Things

The eternally-minded person does not care if he gets a statue erected downtown for pigeons to do their business, but he cares about impacting lives for eternity's sake. And there is no better way to impact lives than those who are closest to you. This concept is where the stay-at-home mom can refocus. She has the opportunity around her knees to shape little lives that will impact eternity. She's doing eternal work in her home as she evangelizes and disciples her children for Christ. Spouses have similar opportunities. We married damaged goods. The fall of Adam hurt our spouses. Poor decision-making and other people also damaged them. One of the most important calls of a spouse's life is cooperating with the Lord in the ongoing restoration of the person they married.

ETERNAL QUESTIONS: How are you cooperating with the Lord in restoring your spouse and children? Have you made ministry or work mistakes?

- A ministry mistake is a person doing ministry out there somewhere but not ministering to their spouse or children.
- The work mistake is the person who is more devoted to their job than to his spouse or children.

Thinking Time

The scattered brain is the bane of our culture. Our world has succeeded in dumbing down our minds to a tweet, quote, infographic, or video clip. Sitting before the Lord lasts as long as the water grab-and-go of a marathon runner. We feed our brains with continuous noise—to the point that there is no such thing as quiet anymore. If there were quiet time, it would be more of a crash time. We're too exhausted to think. We ramp ourselves up to where it's either 100 percent on or 100 percent off. I'm not talking about praying. I'm talking about spending time thinking. You take a thought and roll it over and over and over in your mind like a cow chewing cud until that thought masters you. You take your thoughts captive by bringing them to the obedience of Christ (2 Corinthians 10:3–6). That kind of mental discipline is rare for the post-modern mind.

THINKING QUESTION: Do you have a quiet mind? Like Jesus, can you rest in the storms of your life?

Call to Action

Here are a few ways you can apply these three concepts to your life. Ask the Father to help you to practicalize these ideas into your life. Make it personal to you. These are suggestive preferences, of course.

RISK: Write down three things you'd like to do but don't know how to do them. Maybe it's overcoming a sin pattern, building a relationship, paying down debt, or making a life change. What are those three things?

1. **ETERNITY:** Who are the closest people within your sphere of influence? How do you need to change to help them change? Write down their names and a few bullet points about what you need to do to better position yourself in a cooperative effort with the Lord to serve them.
2. **REFLECTION:** What hinders you from finding adequate time to think? Without becoming a legalist, how can you change this pattern in your life? I changed by journaling, which might not be a good fit for you. The process of writing forces me to stop and think. If you don't learn to stop and think for adequate periods, you will be overcome by the active noise all around you.
3. If you could live your life over again, what would you do differently? Since you are alive, what if you mapped out a plan to do those things? Be specific. Tell a friend.

Perhaps today is a great time to make a decision in faith.

About the Author

Rick Thomas launched the Life Over Coffee global training network in 2008 to bring hope and help for you and others by creating resources that spark conversations for transformation. His primary responsibilities are resource creation and leadership development, which he does through speaking, writing, podcasting, and educating. In 1990 he earned a BA in Theology and, in 1991, a BS in Education. In 1993, he received his ordination into Christian ministry, and in 2000, he graduated with an MA in Counseling from The Master's University. In 2006, he was recognized as a Fellow of the Association of Certified Biblical Counselors (ACBC).

Other Books Available from Life Over Coffee

Boasting in Weakness
Centering Your Marriage on Christ
Communication
Complete Marriage
Don't Apologize
Exchange the Truth for a Lie
Help My Marriage Has Grown Cold
Identity Crisis
Local Church
Loving Me
Mad
Marriage Devotion We Are One
Politics and Culture
Parenting Devotion from Zero to Adulthood
Sex, Temptation, and Modesty
Storm Hurler
The Cyber Effect
The Talk
Wives Leading
You Decide

www.ingramcontent.com/pod-product-compliance
Lightning Source LLC
Chambersburg PA
CBHW052150070526
44585CB00017B/2055